HF5438
0134
White,

Not al
sales
c
                                              2009 11 20

NOT ALL BULL...SMELLS

Sales Points & Personal Motivation Stories

Dick White

Retired Vice President, Sales/Marketing
Oakhurst Dairy
Portland, Maine

authorHOUSE®

AuthorHouse™
1663 Liberty Drive, Suite 200
Bloomington, IN 47403
www.authorhouse.com
Phone: 1-800-839-8640

© 2009 Dick White. All rights reserved.

No part of this book may be reproduced, stored in a retrieval system, or transmitted by any means without the written permission of the author.

First published by AuthorHouse   4/16/2009

ISBN: 978-1-4389-5234-5 (sc)
ISBN: 978-1-4389-5235-2 (hc)

Library of Congress Control Number: 2009902497

Printed in the United States of America
Bloomington, Indiana

This book is printed on acid-free paper.

Table of Contents

Words Of Wisdom 1
Goals With Positive Attitude To Accomplish 3
Qualify Prospects 5
Motivation And Leadership 9
Basic Knowledge Is Not Enough 13
Confidence/Overconfidence/Learning From Failure 17
The Opening And First Impressions 21
Overcoming Objections 25
Be Decisive And Step Up To The Plate 29
When You Are Right, Stand Your Ground 35
Relish Competition—It Keeps You Focused 39
Innovation Makes Things Happen 43
In Life, As Well As Business, The Pendulum Swings 47
Tough And Fearful Decisions—Trust Your Instincts 51
A Salesperson May Be Down, But Never Out 57
No Matter The Size, Take Pleasure In Success 61
Concentrate On The Decision-Maker 67
The Importance Of Empathy 71
Distractions——A Part Of Life 75
Closing And Sound Business 79
Importance Of Prompt Follow-Up 83
Treat Customers Like Gold 87
Determination 91
Leave With A Positive Thought 99

Words Of Wisdom

Life is a story. From the day you are born until the day you die, every living second is unique to you alone. Other people will impact your life, and God only knows how they will try to influence and mold you into what they or society regard as "proper."

Right out of the starting gate, you will be looked upon and judged by all you encounter. "Oh, she or he is such a beautiful and adorable baby!" or "He or she looks just like the mother, father, grandmother, grandfather, or some other person known to the inner circle." In many cases, the truth may be the resemblance to (God forbid) the milkman or some other testosterone-laden individual perhaps known only to the mother.

I am kind of convinced the reason newborn infants begin life with a howl that should shatter most eardrums is because their first experience in the outside world is exposure to a situation where all they can think of is "Where is the delete button?" They're picked up by a stranger with a surgical mask and perhaps hit on the rear, their cord is cut, and they're plopped on a scale, measured, scrubbed, and wrapped in some type of blanket.

Well, enough of that; you are here, for better or worse, and 100 percent dependent on others for immediate survival. The good news is, you are already starting a personal story that no one else can duplicate.

Know it or not, from that huge and important day number one, you have already become a salesman who equals or exceeds the best the world has ever known! As you grow and develop your own unique personality, never again will you command 100 percent attention and have everyone you encounter go out of his or her way to please your every desire; that's a salesman's salesman.

It always concerns me when I hear a person say, "I could never be a salesperson" or "It is just so not me." The following is just a reminder that has been around for a long time. We all sell every day of our lives. The question is how many people will buy? There is not a married person alive who has not used every skill found in any sales manual ever written. Think of all the antics you went through just to get to the altar! The first date … the preparation … the game plan … the strategy … the opening … the dialogue … the listening … the impression … the closing … and the follow through. You both acted the total roles of buyer and seller! You *are* a salesperson every day of your life, like it or not! Now that we have that important fact behind us, I *never* said you were a *good* one!

Goals With Positive Attitude To Accomplish

At the very outset, it was determined that you are a unique individual who is in control of your own destiny. No matter how you are influenced, each day you and you alone process personal thoughts in your brain to everything presented. They require both an action and a reaction. How you file it is up to you. Example: Your boss walks by and comments, "Nice work getting that new account yesterday." You respond with a simple, "Thank you." As you continue down the hall, your thought and brain processes *It was a good pickup; however, if he had let me do it my way, we would have had it a month ago.* No one knows this but you. The boss continues down the hall and perhaps his brain processes *This account will probably be a nightmare and end up costing our firm a fortune.* No one knows but him. My point is this: No matter what you do, it will have an impact somewhere. The important thing is being in control of that impact. If you do not have goals (from the very simple to the very difficult), chances are you will just stumble on through life. If that is your choice, then live with it and be content with the outcome. If you should choose to set consistent easy, mild, and difficult goals, then establish a positive attitude: *Nothing will stand in my way to hinder them from being accomplished.* Know that it will require dedication, hard work, and adjusted completion estimates, setbacks, and that you will most likely experience some disappointments before the goal is complete. Go for it; however, also be realistic. Know that when the goal becomes unrealistic (to the point where achievement gains little or nothing), you have to also know when to bail—with no regrets.

My example of knowing when to bail and accept the outcome is hypothetical; however, if it were to occur, it could be very realistic. Your wife, friend, or significant other has reservations at an expensive restaurant for dinner, followed by dancing at a well-known romantic nightclub. You are well dressed, on your best behavior, and serving wine; she has your full attention. The evening will be fun. In the back of your mind (actually in the front of your mind), you are confident that it will conclude with exciting passion.

While dancing the night away with the foxtrot, cha-cha, tango, or waltz, you are in control and all is well with the world. Just as you are about to call it a night and leave for the real fun, in walks actor Johnny Depp. He never says a word; however, he glances with approval toward your mate and continues on to greet whomever. It is official: Your night is now shot to hell. You are now just an afterthought. Your mate can only focus on calling all her friends to brag that Johnny Depp looked at her with approval. "Oh my God!" she is screaming. "I would love to spend an hour alone with that hunk!"

Just put it behind you. Lick your wounds. After spending all that money, accept the fact: You got dumped by a person who never said a word!

Qualify Prospects

Without a doubt, millions of dollars are wasted every day on decisions we may feel are noble; however, in reality, they are just wasting time. Here is another hypothetical example: A sales manager decides to charter a yacht for an afternoon social and informal get-to-know-you meeting with the executive staff of a new business relocating to your area. It has great potential as a new outlet for your product. Good idea! If the sales manager had done a little research, he would have discovered that the decision-maker had almost drowned the year before and has a deathly fear of boats and the water! The invitations are sent and the charter arrangements are completed, but no one comes! That's a lot of time and money wasted. Trust me; dumb moves like this are very common in the business world. BASIC RESEARCH IS CRITICAL.

We make the same errors in judgment in our personal lives. When my sister and I were young, we looked forward to spending time at the home of Uncle Gus in rural Maine each year. Uncle Gus was old school. He lived on a nice old farm. I think it was the last in the area to introduce electricity and modern plumbing. Getting a telephone was the culmination of an impossible dream; Maine at its best! We loved it. The farm property extended to a river connecting Damariscotta Lake. Uncle Gus enjoyed our visits. He was always in his plaid shirt and suspenders, which were holding up well-worn painter pants. This house was never out of fresh deer meat. The flavor and quality of the meals would put the best of restaurants to shame. When we got older, my sister got her pilot's license and became rated for floats. One beautiful fall day, we took off from our home base at Sebago Lake for a joyride. Why not drop in on Uncle Gus and give him a quick ride, so he could see the lake and farm from the air! Great! We landed on the lake, taxied up the river, beached the plane on the shore, walked the woods trail up to the house, and surprised Uncle Gus. My sister and I were as excited as two kids in a candy store with money to spend. Right off, Uncle Gus could see our enthusiasm and did not have the heart to disappoint my sister! If it had been just me, he probably would have kicked me out of the house. Down through the woods we went, and into the plane climbed my sister and Gus. It was a two-passenger plane, so I stayed behind and pushed the plane onto the river. Twenty minutes later, the plane came back—and out climbed Uncle Gus. He was a new shade of white that I had never seen before or since. He waved goodbye and stumbled up the woods trail toward the house. In the plane, I asked my sister what he thought of seeing the lake and farm from the air. She looked at me and laughed. She said, "I have no idea. From the moment I started the engine, he grabbed onto the seat with both hands and never looked up or released his grip until we stopped at the beach!"

There are times when random prospecting is not only fun but also rewarding. It requires little or no training and the success rate is very high. It is called prospecting and sales by obligation! It can be the annual Girl Scout cookie drive, the grade school student's sale of wrapping paper, or a God-only-knows scheme developed by someone with a plan to fleece the neighborhood sheep!

Motivation And Leadership

I will continue to say it over and over again: "What you become and do with your life is your decision." People can and will have an influence on you in positive and negative ways. In your daily routine, you are like a sponge, absorbing events all around. No matter what you accomplish in life, you possess and exercise both motivation and leadership. To what level you achieve is your choice. Example: As your own children grow, they rely on you for motivation and leadership. Children are very quick to respond with comments like "My mommy or daddy said so," "I have to take out the rubbish before I can come out to play," or "I want to grow up to be just like—" Even if you do not have children, the influence you have on others is enormous!

If your career decision is to work toward a position of responsibility and leadership that involves people reporting to you, it is important to understand that there is a commitment that goes along with the goal. The commitment is to set the best example you can 100 percent of the time. Your attitude and how you conduct yourself in the presence of employees and employers goes much further than many in management realize or accept. Trust and respect are not God-given, they are earned. You are never going to bring out or cultivate the best in others if you are not willing to step up to the plate yourself.

I recall that I was once requested by the local chamber to address the business membership at a luncheon on the general topic of "What are the challenges of being a non-family executive in a family-owned business?"

No problem whatsoever! I was hired to make the family money! When you are hired to do any job, your immediate goal should be to give your employer 100 percent of all you have to offer every moment you are on duty. When you do, things happen! The same is true for the family owners. Employees should not be encouraged to settle for mediocrity, any more than an employer should be considered distant and aloof by the rank and file. You want my best? What are you doing to make sure I have continued security and pride as both an employee and manager?

Every morning, when stepping into the foyer of our building, the very first things I saw were lighted portraits of the founding father of Oakhurst, Stanley T. Bennett, and son, Donald H. Bennett. If you happen to drive by the plant at night and look in, you see the same thing! Talk about intimidation! All I could think of as I climbed the stairs were what their eyes were saying to me: "A lot of people are relying on you; do not screw up!"

By not screwing up, the very first thing you should do is leave all your dirty laundry and personal feelings at the door. When you encounter an employee or other manager, your attitude should be positive. You should have a ready and sincere smile on your face. If I were to walk into the employee room or my office with a sour disposition or a general projection of negative vibes, I can assure you the productivity of the employees decreased 40 percent. *The boss is upset! Does this mean someone may be fired? What have I done wrong?* Conversation at the water cooler, quick interoffice e-mails, and wasted phone calls on company time can add up to a staggering loss. Every employee in the place comes to work daily with some negative cross to carry. The boss does not need to add to the situation.

A good thing to remember as a work ethic is if you give your best and do not like the circumstances, you are free to give a decent notice and go somewhere else. If you have given your best, the good will follow. If you became a general complainer, chances are good that work will become increasingly difficult to find.

The expectation for success of a professional salesman with a negative attitude is like expecting not to get hurt if you insert a glass rectal thermometer designed to shatter over 98.6 degrees!

Basic Knowledge Is Not Enough

It is certainly true that persistence pays off. One can attack a situation time after time. In certain instances, the party may give in with a comment, "I admire your tenacity and persistence." In most situations, you will get kicked out with "Do not ever call me again!" So many sales opportunities are lost because the salesman does not possess adequate product or company knowledge. Why should anyone purchase an item from a person who knows little about the product he is trying to sell? Take whatever time necessary to study and learn all you can about the firm where you work, as well as specifics of products they manufacture or sell. When you have this knowledge, do not try to cram it down the throat of the buyer. Don't try to impress them with how smart you are—unless the prospect asks the questions and wants your input. You can oversell and lose, just as easily as you can undersell and lose. Do not take your skill (or lack thereof) for granted.

The following example of too much information can make my point. I always feel sorry for the foreigner with limited language skills who stops at a fast-food restaurant. This has happened to me. You study the language tape and practice until you are comfortable to proceed. At the counter, you proudly ask for a hamburger. Satisfied that you are about to get a burger, the clerk comes back with (1) How would you like it cooked? (2) Do you want mustard and/or ketchup? (3) Would you like onions? (4) Cooked or raw? (5) Do you want a plain or sesame-seed bun? (6) Fries or onion rings with the order? (7) Small, medium, large? After staring at the clerk with a blank look on your face, you are forced to say, "Just water, please," and you go away hungry!

The following is a true example of being cocky and in control when you really know nothing. At the start of my Oakhurst career (when I was working part time during the summers to pay for college), I started my day at 3:00 AM picking up forty-quart jugs of raw milk from several farms and taking them to the dairy for processing. I then reloaded with milk products and delivered them to summer camps and stores in the Lakes region. I was working alone and was the man in charge, a college kid who knew it all! One morning, I had a note from our quality control lab that a certain cow at one of my farms should be tested for mastitis. I did not even know what it was, much less how to test for it. However, in the glove compartment of the truck was a mastitis test kit. It is simply a litmus test card with four spots on it. One drop of milk was to be applied to each spot from each teat of the cow. It sounded pretty darn simple to me. If she was positive for mastitis, the spot would change color. It was a no-brainer! The owner of the farm, Mr. Edwards, always met me when I stopped at 4:00 AM for pickup. I explained the situation and he said, "Okay, do you want me to do it?"

"No," I said. "Show me the cow and I will take the sample." I had never milked a cow in my life. I sat on the famous wooden stool, placed the card under a teat, and proceeded to pull. Nothing happened. The cow twisted her head around with that *what-the-hell-is-this?* look. I tried again. Nothing happened. Mr. Edwards gave me a word of encouragement, and the next thing, as I recall, a squirt of milk shot out of the teat and soaked the whole card—as well as me! By this time, Mr. Edwards was laughing so hard I knew I would be the subject of Grange Hall meetings and bean suppers for weeks to come! He said, "What do you think?"

Being an embarrassed professional who had to get in the last word, I said, "Appears serious to me—I suggest you beef her!"

Mr. Edwards then took another card and promptly placed one drop on each spot without the slightest effort! Learning the hard way is just fine—provided that you learn.

Confidence/Overconfidence/ Learning From Failure

Again, I state that whatever you accomplish in life is 100 percent up to you. Every day is a learning process that is unique to you alone. The degree of confidence (or lack of confidence) you portray is your issue. You will constantly be bombarded by the you-can-do-it crowd, with similar bombarding from the you-cannot -do-it" crowd. There is a certain amount of truth to both sides. You may be confident; however, not wise to pursue some goals. You may be skilled enough to obtain the goal; however, if you are too overconfident, you may still not get there. There are failure risks with both approaches. This is healthy; to be a success, you must learn that failure can be a great motivator and teacher. We see this in the sports world all the time. Last to first and first to last! Make your own decisions and do not take your eye off the ball.

Here is an example of goal in sight that went south in a hurry: When I was a teenager (under fifteen) and right at the age where girls consumed 80 percent of my focus (the other 20 percent was spent sleeping, so that I could have the strength to support the focus), I enjoyed skiing at Black Mountain in Jackson, New Hampshire. One sunny and warm spring day, I was all decked out in my blue stretch pants, handmade knit sweater, cool goggles, 110 Hart skis with Cub-Co release bindings. I was just trolling for girls to impress with my slope skills. Right beside the T-bar is the steepest section of the mountain, which ended at the base. Everyone who rode the T-bar watched the skiers as they rode up the lift. On the previous run, I had spotted six girls skiing together. I waited at the top of the steep section until I saw them board the lift below. The goal was to wait until they were near and then go into a tuck and schuss the steep slope, so I could pass them flat out, no more than twenty feet from the lift. They would be so impressed that when I caught up with them on the trail, I would be invited to spend the rest of the day skiing with the most beautiful creatures I had seen (since the day before).

Here they came! Quickly, I crouched into my tuck and accelerated down the slope like a bullet. When I was close to them, I could almost hear them exclaim, "Wow, look at him!" I was about to close the sale! In my enthusiasm of the moment, I turned my head to see them. It was a huge mistake to take my focus off the ball at this critical stage. Unprepared, I hit a mogul in the flat light of the day. I launched into space faster and quicker than the space shuttle! Out of control, I crashed face- and chest-first onto the slope. My skis came flying off and I slid for what appeared to be a lifetime. As a positive individual, my first thought was, *At least I will win the sympathy vote for a spectacular wipeout!* What I heard was howls of laughter. At that moment, I began to realize that I was becoming very cold in an area that should be quite warm. I wear glasses. My first priority was to relocate them and regain sight. Thanks to the safety strap still in place, they were perched below my chin and covered with snow. I was getting very cold! Soon I realized that the force of the wipeout ripped not only my blue stretch pants, but also the insulated underwear and my BVD underpants all the way down to my knees. I was naked to the world. This was a problem! How long would it take you to shovel packed snow out from all your undergarments, pull them back up, and proceed down the mountain with some type of dignity still intact?

When you are at the critical part of your presentation, do not take your eye off the ball. Stay focused, close the deal, and get out!

The Opening And First Impressions

There is no doubt that the first impression you make in a sales call (or any first meeting in your personal life) lays the groundwork of future acceptance or rejection. A poor first impression is not impossible to recover from; however, why go to all the trouble when a little effort at the outset will prevent the need to recover? It is very simple to just put yourself in the other person's shoes and attempt to see yourself through their eyes. Do not forget that "what you are is what you get." Way too often, meetings (or any situations) get off to a bad start because the impression is negative. If you wish pursue a sales career, making a positive first impression is a must. There are so many times I would step into the lobby to interview an applicant for a route sales position. What did I find? The person was dressed in baggy, soiled, ripped clothes with hair all askew. Some looked like they were just recovering from a drunk. I did not care what their skill level was at that point; this person was not getting job from me. It shows a total lack of respect. By the time I retired in 2002, the situation was getting so bad, I would have given my position to the first person who showed up with a coat and tie or skirt and blouse!

When I graduated from college in 1967, Oakhurst was a rapidly expanding dairy. I had already worked for them part time since 1959 and enjoyed the business. I was recently married, rated A-1 with the military, and advised that I would receive my official draft notice and would probably be shipped to 'Nam by fall. With my new degree in business and economics, I figured I would work at Oakhurst until drafted, and then pursue some career after military service. I received my notice; however, four weeks before entry, my wife killed a rabbit. Never in wartime did I feel a pregnancy would slow down Uncle Sam. It did, and I was reclassified. When I asked my boss for a reference letter to add to my résumé, he agreed. The next day, when I walked in his office to get the letter, he told me sit down and listen. He had gone to the owner and convinced him that I had all the credentials they were looking for to help expand the company. He asked me if I was interested, and I said yes. He ripped up the letter and the rest is history.

One of my very first sales calls was to the northeastern buyer for the A & P stores, a man by the name of Paul Carey. His office was in Boston and he was known as "the Bear." Paul was a big man who was tough as nails, but he was also very fair to salespeople who knew their stuff. At that time, A & P was one of the largest grocery store chains not only in Maine but the United States. We only served a few stores in the Portland region and were interested in expansion. I was nervous but had rehearsed my pitch many times. When I walked into his office, he did not even stand up to greet me. Instead, he reached for a pendulum-type timer on his desk, set it for three minutes, and basically said something like,

"Young man, I am a very busy individual. You have three minutes to make your pitch and convince me you can help A & P become more profitable!"

I was caught off guard. I completely lost my focus. I sensed very quickly that the standard fastest-growing company with an undisputed reputation for service and quality routine was going to be a total waste of time. So I asked him a question: "What do you regard the most important criteria for dairies who serve your Maine stores?"

He looked me in the eye and said, "Maine is a huge state in our area with very few people per square mile. State law does not give me a price advantage and I feel obligated to support every local company because we cannot feel out of touch with the community.

I know little to nothing about the specific strong or weak points of any of them. I rely on local supervisor advice, which is don't rock the boat."

The timer was about to expire. I thanked him for his comments and left.

On the drive back to Maine, I realized he was right. Few were going to give serious attention to a state so large with a total population smaller than his city! He did not know much about Maine dairies. Neither did I. I had never visited in my life a healthy part of Maine.

Back at the office, I received clearance from my boss to take off for several days and do my own research on every A & P store in the state. I visited every store, posing as a dairy person on vacation out of my competitive area. I was new to the business and wanted their opinions regarding current suppliers. It would help me to develop new skills for use in my own area. Man, did they ever talk! I was handed off to dairy clerks and others who worked the department. I was allowed to take pictures of their cases because I liked the way they were set up; I might try it at home myself. I heard the good and the bad. Each night, I worked on a detailed report of my visits, complete with pictures.

When I was finished with the project, I had firsthand knowledge of the strength and weakness of every dairy in the state, many of which I had never heard about. Most of the data came from the store manager and/or dairy clerk who had to work with them every day.

I called Mr. Carey and requested thirty minutes of his time to review data I felt he would find most interesting. He dove into the report and pictures like it was one of the best Christmas presents he had ever received. It contained no bias at all, as I was not a competitive threat in 80 percent of the area covered. By no means did we become best buddies, but I can say that as we expanded our territory in Maine, authorization for A & P stores was a little less difficult.

Overcoming Objections

You do not have to be a professional salesperson to experience the importance of overcoming objections. If every issue or opportunity you present is shot back to you with some type of objection and you accept it, then you must accept the consequences. As I said, how you process and deal with the daily issues of life is entirely up to you. We are all different with unique, individual minds with which to process and react. Overcoming objections is a normal and daily part of life. If you want to be a professional salesperson (or assume any type of leadership role in your career), this skill must (and will) take on a new level of importance. You must work on it, expect it, and most importantly, learn to deal with it. You can take the stubborn approach ("It's my way or the highway"), the pragmatic approach ("Can we sit down and discuss it?"), or the easy-out approach ("I do not care; just do what you want"). For certain, if you are a married person and do not have the slightest idea regarding the meaning of the expression "yes, dear," you are in for one heck of an interesting marriage.

Understand that in a sales situation, the objections may have a great deal of merit and may be correct regarding the concern of the issue. You do not (and you should not) just give up and write off the prospect as not worth the effort—*not if the ultimate goal is important to you.* You also should never get into an argument to prove your point. In time, it will bite you hard!

Objections can be overcome in the wildest and most unconventional method or methods. Being creative and thinking outside the box is almost a must in certain situations.

The following goal accomplishment is one that remains very close to me. Still relatively early in my career as a sales supervisor, I encountered a group of summer camps in the Casco, Maine region that were not serviced by Oakhurst. We had the majority of these camps, but these appeared unattainable. I served this area summers during my college days and knew the people very well. I knew that Henry Hacker, the owner of Camp Cedar, was the key to the few summer camps we did not service. Every year, I talked and met with him with the same results. "I know you represent an excellent company," he would say. "However, this dairy has served me ever since the camp opened. Their service has been very good. My staff is comfortable with them. They are quite responsive to issues. Because of current price controls, you cannot offer a price advantage. If you were in my shoes, you would also appreciate some loyalty for a job well done."

He was correct on every point. Determined not to leave with my hat in hand and my tail between my legs, I told him, "One day, Mr. Hacker, you will do business with me and I will be able to demonstrate that you are more than just a customer, and we are better than the average dairy." We parted as friends.

In midwinter of that year, we had a freak snowstorm that buried the region with heavy, wet snow. Trees and branches were down and roofs caved in from the weight. It was a real mess and people dealt with no power for quite some time. When the storm ended, I fastened my skis to the car roof, grabbed the camera, and set off for Camp Cedar. I parked the car at the side of the road, climbed up and over a huge snowbank, and skied the quarter mile through the woods to the camp. I was the first one there. I took pictures of all the damage (which was quite extensive) and jotted notes regarding the damage. Mr. Hacker's winter home was in Massachusetts. He, like all others, relied on caretaker staff to look after the camp in winter.

I mailed off the pictures and report with a comment something like "We go the extra mile." A week later, the phone rang. It was Mr. Hacker. He made a comment about how much the family enjoyed the pictures and ended with a statement I will never forget. "Young man, there is nothing else I can say to you other than look me up in the spring and we will have a serious talk." We not only picked up the account, he helped with positive comments to some others, and that season, we had all the camps as our clients.

How you deal with objections is up to you. Do not be afraid to step outside the box.

Be Decisive And Step Up To The Plate

Decisions made in your personal as well as professional life will have an impact on others. One hopes that the majority of those decisions will prove to be positive, but there is no guarantee either way. The important thing to remember is the demand for decision-making will not go away. Many times, it may be wise to make a decision on the spot rather than stall by saying, "This is important and I will have to think about it for a while." A small decision by one may be a gigantic decision for another. Do not forget that you are unique. How your brain processes the subject is yours and yours alone. To one parent, the response to a child's request to spend the night at a friend's house is simple: yes or no. To the other parent, it is as complex a request as deciding whether to change jobs and move to another part of the country! You get my drift. Deal with it, for better or worse. I feel all decisions are made with good intentions. Some just work out better than others.

Instant decision-making is so important that I will give three examples relating to my work career. The first was not so good. The final two had a huge impact on the growth of Oakhurst.

(1) An early-morning milk route stop on my way out of Portland was an account called Spurwink School. It was a home delivery type stop. The rest of my day was large wholesale accounts. Spurwink School housed children who required special attention. That early in the morning, I never saw anyone. I just stocked the refrigerator and left. One morning, a young child walked into the kitchen and wanted to help. I let him put some product away and stack the milk crates by the door. I appreciated the help, so I went to the truck and brought him back a small container of chocolate milk. There were no freebies; I paid for the milk. The morning of my next delivery to Spurwink, a couple days later, I think every child at the school was in the kitchen wanting to help! I was in trouble and I knew it. The bad news was that it cost me more personal money than I could afford. The good news was that the kids were not supposed to be out of bed and the school stopped the situation pronto.

(2) I was at an appointment with the buyer and part owner of Sampson's Supermarkets, Clayte Manson. It was just a routine meeting to establish future promotions for the few stores we served. During the meeting, his private phone rang. He did not like interruptions. Like all good salespeople in that situation, I looked away and pretended not to eavesdrop. When he hung up the phone, I could tell he was livid. He looked at me and asked, "How far down the coast of Maine does Oakhurst deliver?" At the time, it was not very far and I told him the parameters. He told me that a major supplier to one of his largest stores on the coast refused to make a special

delivery on a weekend. The store was going to be out of a key product for nearly a whole day. He asked, "What is required for you to consider future expansion?" The obvious answers included volume, good dairy case position, and enough space so our products would not be hidden or difficult to find. He looked at me and said, "If I authorize you for four of my large stores along the coast, give you your choice of position, and one-third of the total milk space, how fast can you respond?" This was a meeting on a Wednesday. Before he could calm down and rethink the situation, I told him we would start our first delivery the following Monday, providing I was not locked into a time-of-delivery window. He picked up the phone, called the managers of the four stores and a local supervisor, and told them I was coming and that they were to welcome me with open arms!

I immediately went back to the office and met with executive management to explain the situation. We did not have a spare vehicle, much less an employee to serve the route. It was just too good an opportunity to pass up. We had a spare Divco-style home delivery truck that could at least carry enough product for the job. I was very familiar with the skills required for route driver; I said that I would drop all other responsibilities and run the route until we could find and train a replacement. The rest of that week, I visited the stores, met the managers, and determined what was required for product. Early that Monday morning, I set off from Portland to serve four accounts. The most distant was Belfast, which was nearly 100 miles from Portland. I knew we were going to be a quick success when I was stocking the dairy case at Sampson's Rockland store. An old-timer named Walter reached out and picked up a quart of our milk. He said to me, "I have never heard of Oakhurst, but I am going to buy this because it cannot be any worse than the other brands I have had to tolerate." It was not long before Oakhurst became a major seller in the area, and that popularity extends to this day!

(3) I am quite confident there is not an adult alive in the United States who is not aware of Wal-Mart or the popularity they enjoy nationwide. In the early days of their growth, they did not stock dairy products. When they decided to do so, most dairy companies in our area regarded it as a poor decision. I could be counted among those of this opinion until I met a regional supervisor who took the time to explain the early growth goals of Wal-Mart. I was impressed enough to jump on the bandwagon, and promised that we would gladly serve any store they opened in Maine. The early days were rough, to say the least. The stores were very time-consuming, very difficult to serve, and sales were very low for the effort. Route salesmen disliked the concept and work big time! Although sales were slow, they were growing weekly. My long-term projection was positive. By this time, Oakhurst had grown to the point where we also added New Hampshire to our market. At a meeting in Arkansas, we were able to obtain authorization for Wal-Mart's New Hampshire stores as well as the Sam's Club business. It was still very marginal volume for the work and time required. However, by now, I was convinced that this company was about to explode and become a significant player in our whole market.

One day, my phone rang and it was the dairy buyer from Arkansas. We had been performing to their satisfaction, and he was seeking my advice. They needed to find a dairy supplier for their four Vermont stores. He had one more month to have the nationwide program in place, and Vermont was a problem. No one wanted to play. He asked if I had any suggestions to help him, as he was not having much success.

I told him I would put on my thinking cap and call him the next day. I reviewed all I knew regarding Vermont and just could not come up with an idea he had not already attempted. I knew for certain that Wal-Mart was in early preparation to roll out their Supercenter concept nationwide. This move would involve a huge amount of private-label sales. Later that day, I approached Oakhurst owner and CEO Stan Bennett and proposed that we take on the Vermont stores—if in turn we could be given first option of supplying Wal-Mart with private label and our own brand when the opportunity arrived. We were both aware that the expense of covering Vermont was such that it would take a miracle for us to ever become profitable in the state. No matter what the volume, the expense vs. return would not wash.

However, it was first opportunity to supply private label in Maine as well as New Hampshire, and it was a potentially great coup. It would be ours to lose! That very afternoon, I called the buyer back in Arkansas to inform him of the proposal. He fully understood our situation and told me to consider it done—providing we understand that service, quality, and pricing must remain within his guidelines at all times. He asked when we could start serving Vermont. In less than two weeks from the initial call, we had it done and underway. The buyer was pleased. Before it was over, we also obtained the authorization to serve all Wal-Mart stores in eastern Massachusetts. I always had the impression that another major supplier who could have solved the Vermont situation (who had a stronghold in Massachusetts) had said no to Vermont. I feel this did not sit well with Arkansas, but I could be wrong. I probably am wrong; however, my point is to closely study big decisions before you jump. You never know what may come back to hurt or help you later.

When You Are Right, Stand Your Ground

Like it or not, in both your personal and professional life, you will be required to take a side or defend a position. Your choice may be to run from every confrontation and not get involved. If this is the case for you, it is fine. It has become your choice and only you can do anything to adjust the consequences. You may choose not to! You may choose professional help to overcome an issue or issues.

If, however, your career involves a leadership role, taking a stand on any number of issues will be required and you must be consistent. A salesman or leader who has trouble making up his mind will probably find out that he is making few (if any) sales, or those he is trying to lead are rapidly going away. Decisions can be made, pursued, and later determined to be wrong. The wise leader will recognize the error and work to correct the situation. The not-so-wise leader may still lead but find it increasingly difficult. No matter what, you are unique and okay to do it your way.

From the very start of my career, I was given the opportunity to enhance my sales and management skills by attending just about any seminar I chose. I took advantage of several; however, my immediate boss, John Merriman, was the best teacher I encountered. Working with and for him was a pleasure. On-the-job training is often the best way to learn. To me, he was a master.

We had recently expanded into a new sales territory and were determined to become the number-one brand in short order. Most of the total sales in this market were at two well-established local supermarkets. They were important. We needed their business to obtain the goal. We got their business, and progress was slow but steady. One day, the route salesman who served these accounts came into the office on the verge of tears. He was a good man who tried hard to represent us well every day. The problem was that one of the principal owners of the supermarket chain had the habit of appearing at back rooms during receiving. This salesman had no problem with that; however, the owner was going out of his way to give our man a hard time and make him feel foolish to others. The employee asked me what he should do. He was ready to quit.

I approached John for some advice. Right off, he said, "Get an appointment with that owner now!" A few days later, we stepped into his office and I was expecting a battle that would probably get us kicked out of the account. He disarmed the owner immediately. He was never rude; he was, however, able to paint a picture to him that sank in without being offensive. I am confident the owner did not like the issue; however, he agreed that perhaps he was being a little too assertive. We left, still with the business, and the issue with the route man went quietly away. I asked John what he would have done had the meeting gone badly. His reply was that he would have pulled out of the account rather than change a route person—and still have the issue. "Do not forget," John said, "that a dedicated, good employee, trying their best, is better than any single account. If the person is right, stand up for them."

A second example is more recent and relates to Oakhurst Dairy owner Stanley Bennett. About five years ago, the agribusiness giant Monsanto, a St. Louis-based biotechnology company, sued Oakhurst because of what was written on our milk labels: "Our Farmers' Pledge: No Artificial Growth Hormones Used." Stanley had always taken the position that the use of artificial growth hormones was not necessary. We had the farmers who supplied us sign affidavits that they did not use the growth hormone for any milk sold to us. Oakhurst paid them a premium price not to use it. This is very common now, but Oakhurst was the first dairy in the nation to label its milk as hormone-free.

The case was often compared to a David-and-Goliath situation; Oakhurst (and Stanley) became involved in a legal battle that cost his small company a lot of money. The end result was, we could keep the label, but we had to add a disclaimer: "FDA states: No significant difference in milk from cows treated with artificial growth hormones."

The growth-hormone issue has gained a lot of attention during the last few years. It appears that a significant percentage of the population agrees with the Oakhurst position (that they are not necessary). When some of the largest retail giants came out with the statement that they would not purchase private-label products containing growth hormones, it really had an impact on the industry.

This suit gained national recognition and publicity. Today, the Monsanto Company has divested itself from the controversial dairy hormone business. In some part, whether small or large, Oakhurst probably played a role in the decision. When you feel you are correct, stand up to the plate to be counted!

Relish Competition—It Keeps You Focused

At some point early in life, most children dream of becoming a professional athlete, fighter pilot, astronaut, or any number of recognized professions, which are exciting and known to all. For the majority, the desire goes away and they become focused on other achievements. The fact one enters an arena of their choice is the important criteria. The athletes who excel to a level of national recognition are few among many. There are thousands in every sport who give it their best 24/7 and are likely never to be known outside a very small circle. They are all winners.

No doubt, there are individuals who have been awarded every material thing desired in life. Their personal circumstance may allow for it. This is not my focus. One may have all the material things desired. Goals that require competition are healthy. It could be anything. A personal competition may be to have the best- waxed vehicle in the neighborhood, or the best-trimmed lawn. Be the best cribbage player on the block. I am confident you can compete with something. Discover it and make it happen.

Dick White

When it comes to flowers, caring for them to become their best is a real art and talent. What I know about flower specifics is borderline embarrassing; however, when I see beautiful plants, I am impressed.

I am very proud of my wife and her dedication to raising flowers in the house as well as a delightful flower garden in our yard. She devotes hours per week to the task, and the results are amazing. Talk about not being afraid to compete. She is a wonderful example of what I mean.

The Philadelphia Flower Show (the first week of every March) is the oldest and largest indoor flower show in North America. Talk about competition! For the week, the show will attract nearly 500,000 people. They come from all over the world to see the best of the best. There are dozens of commercial landscape scenes, complete with full-grown trees, waterfalls, ponds, buildings, and settings so real, one would swear you were walking a trail in the woods or standing in an outdoor garden. Nothing artificial is allowed in the building.

The show covers ten acres of floor space. A large portion is devoted to potted-plant classes. There are multiple entries in each, with all plants judged for ribbons by experts in the category. One should understand that even if a plant does not receive a ribbon, the owner is a winner. This is because the show is so important and competitive that each and every entry is pre-examined by an expert and must pass a basic examination before it is even allowed to be displayed.

The judging is very fair, and done by a small group of people highly qualified for the particular class. Each group assigns point values to each plant, and the ribbons are determined by highest total. In no way do the judges know who owns the plant being judged, as the data on the card with this information is upside down by the plant and not to be overturned until judging is complete.

Once a plant wins a blue ribbon in novice class, the owner can no longer enter this type of plant in novice. They are forced into the general class, where they compete with the best of the best. My wife only grows plants for competition in our home using a plant stand set up for special lighting and a fan for air circulation. Her cacti are grown on a standard garden window in our breakfast room. She is competing with several people who not only own or have specially designed greenhouses, but many also employ a staff just to care for their plants.

She first entered the show in 1997. She did not win a ribbon the first year; however, determined to improve, she tackled the issue head-on and won a red ribbon with an orchid in 1998. Soon after, she was winning blue ribbons in novice. On she moved to the general class. She has won blue, red, yellow, and honorable mention with a variety of plants in general class. Every year, the competition becomes increasingly fierce; however, she always seems to win something!

In 2007, she won several ribbons. At our New Jersey home, the local paper, the *Daily Journal*, visited our home, conducted an interview with my wife, and snapped several photos. On the front page, they posted a notice that she would be featured in an article later that week. It was great!

Oakhurst Dairy is an excellent example of a small third-generation family-owned business competing with giants of the industry. In the 1960s, there were more than fifty processing dairies in Maine. Today, the number with significant size and volume has been reduced to three. With sales around 100 million, Oakhurst competes with other firms whose sales range from 1 to 10 billion!

It may not have the "deep pockets" and resources of billion-dollar firms; however, it does have a positive reputation with consumers that is unsurpassed. I have already discussed the no-artificial-growth-hormone issue. The family-owned business believes strongly in the support of children, community, and environmental programs. So much so, it devotes 10 percent of its profits to kids and the environment. Recently, it has assigned several route vehicles to operate with bio-diesel fuel. Also, the dairy is installing solar panels to help reduce dependence on oil. The list goes on and on. In Maine, the firm is so well known for its quality and community support that Oakhurst-branded milk sales are number one in the state. I am quite confident that if you were to stop a Maine native on the street and ask them to name the first dairy company that comes to mind, it would be Oakhurst. This type of customer loyalty and trust comes from the family desire to compete with anyone and always give back. Stay competitive. Stay focused.

Innovation Makes Things Happen

Thinking through a problem or situation and coming up with a plan or idea that works is often required to close a sale as well as overcome difficult hurdles. When faced with a difficult situation, playing the "be creative game" can yield awesome results.

The rapid technological changes in the dairy industry (or any industry) can often leave one buried, as they come very fast. Change often means getting it done now in order to remain competitive. The dairy industry is not one that allows you to coast.

In short order, I witnessed our industry shift from glass to paper to plastic. It seemed like you were just getting a handle on one when it was soon to go away!

One example of plant innovation under pressure goes back to the time we were converting from mostly paper products to plastic. The company was expanding rapidly. We had just converted our conveyor belts to handle high-speed filling of plastic bottles. Problem—we were having a major issue getting the labels to stick properly. The center was fine, but the edges were not sticking completely.

Earlier, I mentioned admiration for my first immediate boss, John Merriman. As the business progressed, John shifted his skills from general sales manager to plant manager. I replaced him as general sales manager.

Like all good managers, John contacted experts and engineers in the industry for plant visitations and advice to quickly solve the issue. As I recall, the lowest cost estimate to correct the situation was so high, any budget consideration would be blown out the window. The expense was too great and could not be done.

John simply sat back and determined the problem could be easily fixed with little expense. Next thing we knew, he returned to the plant from a local hardware store with some paintbrushes! With some staff help, he went to the machine shop and soon had rigged the paintbrushes to a tension spring on the conveyor belt.

As the bottles with marginal label application proceeded along the line, they passed the paintbrushes with adjusted tension. Labels now adhered completely. Problem solved! Total expense including labor and material: well under $200. Obviously, the plant did not continue long term with paintbrush technology. It bought time needed to correct the problem in a rational and cost-effective manner.

Another innovative marketing program (that proved to be highly successful) was suggested by second-generation owner and president (now deceased) Donald H. Bennett. Nearly every firm uses coupons for their product as one method of promotion. As babies consume gallons of milk, the new mom and dad are wonderful prospects. Don knew the strain on the budget of most new families was very high. His program was a system where every newspaper in our marketing area was scanned daily for new births. Each family of a newborn received a coupon in the mail with a short congratulatory note. The coupon was for ten dollars and could be redeemed at participating grocers. The coupon had *no strings* attached. It was not at all tied to milk (or even restricted to our brand of milk) but could be used toward any store purchase. Kind of "help to get you started," as we know ten dollars might be of great use. I was sales manager at the time and cannot think of another promotion we tried that brought such a positive response. The positive phone calls and letters were numerous. It also gained Oakhurst new and loyal consumers. When determined and focused, you can compete with anyone.

In Life, As Well As Business, The Pendulum Swings

There is one thing in life that cannot be avoided any more than death or taxes. It relates to change. Every moment of your life, circumstances are changing all around. Like it or not, we constantly age. Also, modern technology refuses to let us stand still.

Life, business, and sales are like a pendulum. None remains static. You may choose to sit back and just smell the roses. This is fine; however, also understand that the season will change and the rose will go away. It will return, but never as the same rose. The next one may be more beautiful or just plain ugly.

Thinking of life as a pendulum forces one to plan for change. You may have closed the largest sale of your life and have every right to be thrilled and celebrate. If you are not laying immediate plans to keep the buyer satisfied, I assure you the day will come when it will all go away.

When the pendulum is on the upswing, use this time to plan for when it is going to start back down. The good and bad force you to plan and accept change. When you are stuck in a rut, comfortable, and content with everything, start preparing to be shocked. You are unique. How you deal with any situation is up to you. When complacent with the same old routine, it may take a shock to get you refocused.

A humorous example of being comfortable with status quo reminds me of a true incident that occurred when I was a young supervisor.

It was one of my responsibilities to assure each route left the dairy each day for its appointed rounds. You must understand that in the dairy business, all routes go out as planned. The cows are going to be milked daily, no matter what the circumstances. In the milk business, a blizzard, hurricane, or horrible condition is just another day. For some reason I will never understand, when weather conditions are projected to be bad, people flock to the store and clean them out of milk and bread. Bread is perhaps okay, but what good is the milk if you have lost your power and the refrigerator is off limits? In poor conditions, our industry gets very busy.

At the time, I was in charge of about thirty routes. Sunday was truly my only day of rest, as it was our only down day. With thirty routes, you could count on the fact the phone would ring in the middle of the night with some excuse why one could not go to work that day. Our routes left the dairy between 2 and 5 AM.

By choice, our only phone was in the hallway. With late-night calls, I did not want to disturb my wife or three young children. I was very alert and focused. I could be out of bed in complete darkness, cross the bedroom, open the door, turn left, proceed up the hallway, and answer it by the third ring!

One night, it rang and at full bore and in total darkness, I jumped to my same old routine. Why turn on lights and disturb the whole house? Slight problem: That day, my wife had re-adjusted the bed and furniture in the bedroom, and stupid me did not take it at all into consideration. Immediately, I crashed at full speed into our walk-in closet and found myself thrashing around the clothes like a bull in a china closet. It was not funny, as the next thing I recall, I kicked a chair with my bare foot, and to this day I still laugh over screaming, "I broke the webbing between my little and next toe!" I do not know what you really call it and I know I am not a duck.

The phone was still ringing. Foot bleeding, I found my way out of the room and to the phone. My wife was up and going into a slight tirade because the kids were now awake and crying. She calmed down and went into fits of laughter when I explained the webbing incident.

Moral: When you remain complacent, witness circumstances shift around you, choose not to immediately adjust, be prepared to accept the "stupid."

Tough And Fearful Decisions— Trust Your Instincts

    Again, I remind you that when you bounce ideas off of others, you will receive all kinds of well-meaning advice. People can be very forceful in the wisdom of their counsel. When you are the leader, the final choice will be yours. The issue may be perceived as small in importance. When this is the case, no matter the outcome, there is not much damage to the whole. However, the issue may be huge. It could result in significant losses or even personal injury. Seek all the advice you want; however, at the end, trust your own instinct. If you are not comfortable, chances are the goal will not be reached. A certain amount of fear should and will sharpen your focus.

    The following personal goal includes several of the skills required to complete any sale. It will also demonstrate how a healthy fear will keep you focused.

    Mountaineering has been a hobby of mine since childhood. Rarely have I seen a happy jogger. With sweat pouring off of them, the strain on their faces gives the appearance of pure agony. I prefer getting exercise by tossing a pack on my back and heading for the mountains. Most of my hiking and climbing has been in the White Mountains of New Hampshire. To this day (I am sixty-six and still at it) a group of close friends and I head off in winter for a couple overnights and days enjoying the back woods of the White Mountain National Forest. We sleep in unheated bunkhouses at well below zero degrees. We hike, climb, and eat so well, we weigh more when we come out than when we started. One should experience mountains in winter to appreciate their true beauty.

When in my sixties, I bowed to the pressure of entering my second childhood. To most people who know me well, it was entering my fifteenth or greater second childhood! I had watched ice climbers on sheer walls (complete with ice axe, crampons, ice screws, climbing rope, harness, carabiners, slings) and was fascinated by the prospect. I decided that learning to climb ice was next on my agenda.

In late winter of 2002, I contacted EMS Climbing School in North Conway, New Hampshire. Soon I had an appointment to meet climbing instructor and guide Kevin Mahaney. Early one winter morning, we set out for a popular ice slope called Willey Slide in Crawford Notch. Willey Slide is the result of an avalanche that tragically engulfed an entire family around 1856. The slide left behind a very long and large expanse of steep, bare rock. In winter, it completely ices over and is an excellent challenge for ice-climbing beginners. To an experienced ice climber, Willey Slide is like an intermediate downhill ski slope. They practice on it before tackling a real challenge. To me it was the steepest and scariest wall of ice I had ever seen. Before we roped up and got serious about climbing several pitches to the top, I was instructed and had to complete several falls in various positions on a steep slope to prove I could "self-arrest" to the instructor's satisfaction. Self-arrest means purposely falling (sliding) down a steep slope, quickly getting into proper position, and using your ice axe to stop yourself before accelerating out of control. This is serious business. If not done quickly and accurately, you could plunge to the bottom and risk very serious injury or death. I was an eager student and determined to master the skill to the best of my ability. After several falls from various positions and self-arrests, Kevin decided I was okay to proceed.

With our climbing harness secure, we roped in and started up the slope. Plant the ice axe above your head. Kick into the ice with the front point of your crampon, and head on up! Kevin went first, and stopped every twenty feet or so to insert an ice screw into the slope, fasten a carabiner to the ice screw, feed the climbing rope through the carabiner and lock it, and then proceed with the climb. Why the ice screws? The reason is simple: If you are the lead climber and were to fall, in theory you would not fall further than double the distance you are from any given carabiner and ice screw. The ice screw will stop your descent via the climbing rope becoming taut and the person below acting as anchor or "belay." Hope to hell this never happens! If you fall ten feet above an ice screw, you should fall not more than twenty feet.

Climbing ropes can be of different lengths and construction. Mine was 160 feet long. As the lead climber ascends, they periodically stop to allow the climber below to climb up to them. As the lower climber comes up, they stop to retrieve the ice screws and carabiners along the way. You only have a fixed length of rope. Each rope length is called a "pitch." Thus, you keep on going, and all is well and exciting with the world!

When you reach the top or however high you determine to go, it is time to come back down. It does not bother a lot of climbers; however, I can assure you that I rarely (if ever) look down the slope.

How do you go back down? Very easily. You rappel. This technique is actually a lot of fun. I love to rappel, and find the whole experience exciting.

The climbing rope is 160 feet long and you may be 700 feet up the face. You simply secure the rope where you are, halve it and toss it eighty feet down the slope. The rope is fastened to your harness by a device called a "Super 8" or an ATC. Down you go at whatever speed you feel comfortable. With the rope attached to the Super 8 or ATC, you can easily control your descent. These are locking devices, which you can easily control with one hand. They work so well, one could just hang in midair, using no more pressure than what you may exert on the rope with a finger. After you descend the rope length, you secure yourself to the ice wall with another screw, sling, and carabiner, and then pull the rope through until it drops to you from eighty feet above. You then repeat the process until you are safely down the slope. It is kind of scary, but doable. Right? Let me tell you the really scary part.

I said when you started down, the rope must be fastened at the top, and after you descend eighty feet, the rope is pulled through and the process repeated. This is great; however, if you leave behind an ice screw (very expensive) and a carabiner (fairly expensive), the descent would become quite expensive! When I confronted Kevin with this expense, he said something like "Are you crazy? No way do we waste or leave ice screws and carabiners on the mountain."

"Well," I said, "we are on a sheer wall. How do we secure the rope for the descent?"

Then came one of the few times in my life that I have been completely frightened, nervous, and scared. Kevin simply reached in his pocket and removed a string of what resembled leather, not much thicker than a bootstrap. It looked like a piece of rawhide. I believe it is really called a V-thread. He then proceeded to take an ice screw and screwed it into the ice at an angle. He then backed it partway out, then about six inches to the side of the hole, screwed another one in again until it intersected the first hole. He backed out both screws, inserted the V-thread into one hole with a loop tied at the end. With the V-thread in as far as it would go, he inserted a wire with a hook on the end, captured the V-thread, and pulled it through. He then tied off the V-thread, passed half the climbing rope through it, and tossed it all down the face of the slope. He fastened his ATC to the rope, leaned back, and started to rappel down. He said, "When I am down, you clip onto the rope and follow." Total cost of the cord was under a dollar. I can honestly tell you, I was frightened. He quickly calmed me by saying, "Look, I do this for a living. I want to get home safely each day, same as you." The V-thread is pressure tested to hold more than 2,000 pounds. He also reminded me that three inches of good ice on a lake would hold up an automobile. The secret was and is the quality of the ice. He was not about to put our lives on the line with poor ice. The first twenty feet down the rope, I was as frightened and nervous as I have ever been in my life. Soon after that, it became old hat.

In this experience, I was afraid; however, the goal was accomplished because I became so focused on every move, and there would be no error. Later on, I hired Kevin to lead me on one of the most classic ice climbs in New England. It is called Pinnacle Gully, and it is located in Huntington Ravine on Mount Washington, Pinkham Notch, New Hampshire. To this day, I enjoy the thrill and have memories for a lifetime.

Healthy fear will lead to increased self-confidence. Self-confidence is a must for continued success in sales. Trust your instincts and go for it!

A Salesperson May Be Down, But Never Out

This may be an inaccurate observation on my part; however, it appears that when in the company of other salespeople, or just in the company of any people, the conversation centers around some type of success by whoever "has the floor" at the time. To me, this is extremely healthy and uplifting. To hear the story of the individual who won $2,000 at the casino (but never mentions the countless thousands lost prior to that) makes you want to run for the blackjack table. The man in control at the bar who is expressing in detail how he bedded some well-known fair maiden makes your loins stir with envy at the thought. Truth being, he probably "lost it" before her pants were down! The lady at the bar who smiles at you and exposes a little cleavage makes you end up buying her several drinks, and you still go home alone! Who cares? At times it is fun to live in a "what could have been" world.

In sales as well as personal life, you do not close every sale or win every discussion. Be thankful you are able to live to see another day! Today, you just might!

From time to time, when you have just received uncalled-for rejection, the day may end on a positive note.

The following story is true. I do not recall the specific dates; however, they are not important. I have already made the point that as general sales manager of the dairy, I was able (and often required) to attend seminars and conventions relating to our business.

It just so happened that at this period of time in my life, I was also single. I was chosen to represent our firm at a very important conference at one of the world's premium resorts in West Palm Beach, Florida. I am not going to name it, because I firmly believe that my personal feelings or interests should in no way project a negative connotation toward an excellent establishment.

Anyway, the conference was great; however, for a single person of my age, this place was the most boring spot on the planet! In the evening, the elderly played bridge and discussed where else in the world they were going the following week to do the same thing! The excitement was watching the local rescue unit arrive to cart off whoever had neglected to take their digitalis pill!

Thank the Good Lord, the second-generation owner of Oakhurst, (Don Bennett) had a winter apartment home not too far from the resort. Although I worked for him as a non-family member of the business, we became friends and I enjoyed visits with him and his wife Terri.

One afternoon, at the conclusion of a "conference day," I called Don and was invited to visit for a chat and some drinks. There is a God! Get me out of this place! After a wonderful evening (and a few toddies) it was time to head back to the resort. I still remained wide awake and did not want to return. I asked Don if he knew an area of the city that contained nightclub dancing. He had no specifics, but at least gave the name of a street he thought had some clubs.

Off I went, and I was soon hitting them all! I was looking for a place to dance, not just drink. For good exercise, I love to dance. Not having much luck finding a dance club well after 1 AM, I spotted a place with promise. Big mistake! I had on a decent shirt and a tie. When I first walked in, visibility was about zero. I kind of felt my way to the bar, climbed up on a barstool, and ordered my favorite cocktail—gin and tonic. That was also a mistake. As my eyes became accustomed to the light, I soon realized I was in a biker bar, where an overdressed person had on a T-shirt with a pack of cigarettes rolled up in the sleeve. Also, everyone in the place drank beer straight from the bottle!

The situation was not looking good, and was about to get worse. The barmaid returned with my G&T and flatly stated a price around $10.00. This barmaid (I believe) was also a professional arm wrestler. I reached for my wallet, and much to my chagrin, the smallest bill I had was a fifty! This was so long ago, one traveled with cash and traveler's checks. If credit cards were around, they were out of my league.

I handed her a fifty-dollar bill and stated clearly what it was. In time, she returned with change for a twenty, a five and five singles, expecting a tip. I said "Miss, I gave you a fifty-dollar bill."

She said, "No, it was a twenty."

I said, "No, it was a fifty."

About this time, the drunk beside me (who probably rolled over tanks with his bare hands for exercise) stated, "The lady said it was a twenty.

I quickly sized up the situation and said, "You are probably right—keep the change."

Talk about depression and lost opportunity! It cannot get much worse than this. Very discouraged, I headed back to the fancy resort. By now, it was close to 3 AM. I had accomplished nothing and had just gotten fleeced!

I entered the huge lobby and was slowly working my way toward an elevator when I noticed a person staring at me. It was a fairly young night custodian who was mopping the floor. He said, "Excuse me, sir, are you a guest in this hotel?"

I probably muttered some dumb remark like, "I'm afraid so."

He became very excited. He walked up to me like I was a famous movie star or similar person of interest. His comment was something like he had worked at the resort late nights and had never seen a guest. He was excited and overjoyed to be talking with a person he perceived as being wealthy enough to stay in such a place. He asked if I would do him the honor of allowing him to open the elevator door for me! Can you believe it? All of a sudden, I have gone from a frustrated, fleeced, and angry loser to a person of high esteem!

You know, I went to my room feeling pretty good with myself, as I knew he would be relating to many how he had the privilege of meeting and talking with the guest of a world-famous resort.

One of my favorite books relates to a man who tried, yet constantly met with disappointment and failure. Within two years, his life changed and he was catapulted to president of the United States. The book was written by Dale Carnegie and is called *Lincoln the Unknown*.

Failures and rejections are only a part of life. What you do and learn from them is what matters. You are unique. How you deal with the positive and negative is your story. I like the expression, "Just deal with it!"

No Matter The Size, Take Pleasure In Success

How do you measure success? One person's statement of success may be interpreted as a failure or unimportant by another. No matter what the issue, do not let others rob you of a personal victory. When you have accomplished something positive in your life, take some personal time to reflect and enjoy the feeling. Every success story becomes a building block for greater self-confidence: The first time the teacher randomly called on you for an answer and you got it right. The day you passed a road test, entering a new dimension of importance in your life. The day you graduated from high school or college and were not anywhere near the top of your class. You get the picture! The success was important to you. How others perceive it is their issue. A personal tip: Enjoy the success; however, do not dwell on it so long that others cannot stand to be around you. Remember—it is just as bad to oversell as undersell.

My personal story regarding a major success for me yet little or nothing to those in the know once again involves climbing.

The ice-climb lessons are now behind me. Now I have an urge to put the new skills to a personal challenge. Most of my hiking and climbing friends are content with their level of expertise at mountaineering. They are all excellent in the mountains. Hiking and climbing with them is a pleasure. They support my enthusiasm regarding more challenging mountain goals; however, I think they feel I am a little out of it, and remain content to sit back and watch the "idiot" proceed.

Mount Washington is by far my favorite stomping ground when it comes to hiking and climbing. At 6,288 feet, it is the highest peak in the northeastern United States. First climbed by Darby Field in the summer of 1642, today thousands of people reach the summit yearly via automobile, cog railway train, or hiking/climbing.

On the surface, it does not seem like much of a mountain or much of a challenge. Wrong! Because of its location, Mount Washington experiences some of the worst weather conditions recorded in the world. The summit happens to be located at the intersection of two upper-air jet streams. On April 12, 1934, the summit surface station recorded a wind gust of 231 miles per hour! The record still stands to this day. Hurricane force winds can and often do occur weekly at the summit. By the turn of this century, more than 128 documented people have lost their lives on its slopes; not a mountain to be taken lightly. In winter, temperatures of forty degrees below zero (and hurricane winds) are not that uncommon.

Having the experience of two ice climbs behind me, I felt the urge to tackle a steep slope on my own.

Central Gully in Huntington Ravine is a beautiful sight to behold. It can easily be seen from the main highway near the Appalachian Mountain Club base lodge at Pinkham Notch.

The entire left side of the gully consists of a rock cliff. The right side is not so daunting; however, the combination of the two yields a gully in the middle that is several hundred feet long and quite steep. The degree of steepness ranges from forty to fifty-five degrees. At its base, Central Gully spreads out onto a boulder-strewn area called "the Fan."

Early one April morning, I set out with my climbing gear and the determined goal to solo Central Gully. When I say early, it means on the base fire trail and hiking by 5 AM. It is about a two-and-a-half-mile hike to the bottom of "the Fan" at Huntington. I wanted to be at the base of Huntington early to plan my strategy for the assault. In the early morning hours, the snow pack is most solid because of the extremely cold nights. Later in the day, as the sun rises, the heat from the sun will soften the snow. Soft snow on a steep slope is much more likely to avalanche than hard-packed frozen snow.

The temperature was in the middle teens and quite pleasant for climbing. The sky was overcast; however, the visibility in the ravine was excellent. Although the wind above the ravine on the Alpine Garden trail was forecast to be around forty miles per hour, it was not an issue in Huntington. My plan was to climb Central and then hike the Alpine Garden to the intersection of the Lion's Head winter trail. The winter trail would be descended back to the fire trail and Pinkham base lodge.

Snow conditions were excellent. Hard packed, but not solid enough to require using crampons. I could get by using my ice axes and "kick-stepping" steps into the snow. Also, there was little danger of post-holing! When you post-hole, your foot sinks into the snow up to your knee or further, and continued climbing demands a lot of extra work and energy.

Dick White

I also brought along my camcorder to film this whole event. At the top of the Fan, the base of Pinnacle Gully is on the left. I stopped and recorded a lot of Pinnacle, as less than two weeks before, Kevin had guided me up this classic ice climb. We ended that day with a rappel from top to bottom. One of the many highlights of my life!

Pushing on, I entered the base of Central Gully. From here on up, the gully became increasingly narrow and steep, to the point where you could kick a foothold in the snow and easily reach out with your hand and touch the slope before you. Well I was taking *no* chances and was also using both ice axes. I was alone on the mountain. The view was and is spectacular.

After stopping several times to film and drink in every moment of the experience, I looked up and was nearing the top of the gully, where it flattens out onto the Alpine Garden. Thrilled beyond description and so proud of myself for nearing the end of a major event, I felt I was feeling a bit like Edmund Hillary must have felt when about to summit Everest!

Right at this minute of personal euphoria, I heard the sound of kick-stepping below me. I glanced down, and coming up the slope like a racehorse just out of the gate was another climber. By itself, this was fine; however, he also had a set of skis propped over one shoulder! Quickly, he caught up to me and we both moved to the side of the gully to rest and chat on a boulder. I said something like, "Skiing in forty-mile-per-hour winds above the alpine garden is not going to be much fun in weather like this!"

He replied with a chuckle, "I am not going to the Alpine Garden. I am about to stop, put on my skis, and descend Central Gully."

Talk about bursting a bubble! Man, was my ego ever deflated in a hurry. I took the camcorder out of my pack to film the show. Tom was an attorney from Portland, Maine who moved here from Colorado. While in Colorado, he was known as an extreme skier, or one who routinely jumped off high cliffs with skis, and shoots down nearly vertical slopes with reckless abandon. I said, "This is a long, steep, icy, and narrow gully. No room to maneuver!"

He shrugged his shoulders and stated that he considered this run to be an intermediate challenge. I was polite, but inwardly wanted to kill him.

Sure enough, he donned his skis and then proceeded to lean sideways down the fall line of the slope and started making the most beautiful jump turns I had ever witnessed. He continued in this fashion until the slope widened out a little, and then shot to the base like he was fired from a cannon.

It took a lot of wind and thunder out of my ego; however, it did little to reduce my feeling of a goal well accomplished.

Your first sale may appear of little or no value; however, it is and should be as important to you as the largest sale you ever make. Treat *every success* like a building block to bigger and better things.

Concentrate On The Decision-Maker

Whether in personal or professional life, just stop to reflect on all the time wasted by pursuing a goal that ended up with a "no sale" because you wasted time and energy in the wrong direction.

For some unexplained reason, we seem to feel that every thought and idea is brilliant and should be quickly embraced by all. Remember, you are a unique individual and personal thoughts are yours to keep, no matter what the outcome.

You may reflect back on the days you were young and no one understood. A group of friends want to go to the beach on Saturday. Your parents have the only vehicle that might be available for the outing. With your friends, you lay detailed and specific plans for the day: Pick-up at 7 AM. Breakfast at Denny's. Quick stop at the mall for necessary beach supplies. Where to meet other friends. What time you will head for home. The planning list goes on and on, and the whole group is now excited.

At home, you discuss the whole idea with your brother or sister. They feel it is great and sounds like a lot of fun. When you approach your parent or parents with the whole scenario, you have already invested hours in preparation. The whole thing quickly becomes a flat-out NO. End of the line. No further discussion.

You get the idea. No matter what the idea or thought, it was not going to happen without the blessing of the real decision-maker or -makers. Perhaps the same amount of time would have been better devoted by planning and making your pitch to the person or persons in control of the car keys.

In this case, you may have needed an ally of one parent helping you convince the other that the idea was sound and okay. Springing it on them after the fact was not a sound approach.

It pays to be a perceptive person when it comes to locating the *real* decision-maker. It may not be an owner, spouse, department manager, or anyone with actual authority.

My personal story regarding the "real decision-maker" relates to my general sales manager days at Oakhurst.

We had just introduced a new product to our line and determined it would be wise to devote personal management time for visits to key customers on each route. This would show personal interest and place persons in authority at the customer level. After all, many accounts felt persons in charge at the office were too lazy to get out from behind the desk to make a personal visit. They would much rather send a flyer with all the specifics.

I assigned all the supervisors a group of routes with specific customers to visit and arrange for the new product to be ordered, and to determine shelf space and placement of point-of-sale material.

I chose to visit customers on a route that covered my "old college days" territory. Many of the stores were still owned by the same people. I knew the area well and looked forward to visiting with some old friends again.

For several years the route had been covered by a legend in our company named Norm Sanderson. I can honestly never recall him missing a day of work. Norm was also from the old school, and was very set in his ways. Customers loved him. He knew them all by name, as well as their entire families. He was truly considered a family member by most. In all the years I managed, I could count on one hand the complaints received from his customers.

In I went to customer after customer. I was now known in the area as the "big boss." Customers were pleased to see me. We spent a lot of time chatting about the old days and changes in the industry. I was having so much fun, it seemed a shame to know I was getting paid for this much enjoyment! Customers were eager to see and learn about the new product. When it came time to place an order as well as determine shelf space, I received the same reply time after time: "Dick, we know this is a good product and probably going to sell quite well; however, regarding whether or not I buy it or determine where it should go, I am going to discuss it with Norman. If he thinks it is a good idea, he can do whatever he wants."

I was the general sales manager! At the time, the only persons in the dairy with higher authority were the vice president of sales (Jim Tabor) and the owner. If they had gone into the same accounts, the answer would have remained the same.

So much for spending two full days of my time and accomplishing little more than fun visits with old friends. When Norman arrived at the plant one day, I went to his truck for a chat. Calling a man of his ability to my office (to me) would have been an insult. Meeting on his turf was the correct approach. We talked and laughed about my experiences. When it was all over, Norm simply said, "I'll take care of it."

Selling the wrong person may be fun for you and a great ego- builder; however, *perceptive advanced planning* will yield great results with less effort. You may not be able to get to the real decision-maker early on; however, be creative in your discussions with the advance team until you reach the goal.

The Importance Of Empathy

Quite frequently, you will hear the expression, "Do not criticize the person until you have walked in their shoes or moccasins." Do not take this expression lightly, as there are many instances where empathy will be a real door-opener. It is easy to put this off with the expression, "I dislike moccasins," or "Their shoe size is a ten and I wear a twelve." Be a wise guy all you want; however, the person who is able to project real and sincere empathy in a presentation will probably close more sales than the standard pitch guy.

I am not going to belabor this point; however, I want to share a story where some empathy created an opportunity for my dad that he never felt he could or would attain.

As a child, our family home was at Sebago Lake. At nearly forty-six square miles, Sebago is the second-largest lake in Maine. The Spaulding Estate was on the western shore of the lake, owned by Mrs. Spaulding (not related to Spaulding sporting goods). Our family was invited one day each summer as her guests. Not only did we have the run of the estate, but we also enjoyed a lake cruise on her private yacht. At that time (the late 1940s), the yacht was the largest vessel on the lake.

One day I asked my dad how we were so fortunate to get this annual invitation. What he told me made the famous Dale Carnegie line "Don't criticize, condemn, or complain" truly come to light.

Dad worked his whole career at an Oldsmobile/Cadillac dealership in Portland, Maine. He was there during the Great Depression. How I hated hearing the story over and over again about walking five miles to work to save the five-cent trolley fare. That was after walking two miles delivering morning papers. I wanted to say, "Invest in a bike," but never did.

One day, the widow Spaulding drove her car to the garage, complaining of a noise. Not being able to understand what a "thingamajig" or "whatchamacallit" was, Dad invited her to go on a test drive with him to hear for himself.

The roads in the 1930s were not that great. Knowing that he would have to drive at a variety of speeds to determine the problems, he simply asked Mrs. Spaulding if the speed and quick changes would bother her. She said, "Thank you for asking; the speed would not be an issue."

A few weeks later, the owner of the company called Dad into his office for some news that would leave him speechless. Mrs. Spaulding was soon to take a tour of the United States with friends in her Caddy limo. Her chauffeur was unable to make the trip. She was so impressed with Dad for having asked her feelings regarding speed while on the road test, she wanted him to chauffeur them. He would be fully compensated, as well as all expenses covered while gone. The company owner was not to put his position in jeopardy at all while away. What is the owner going to say to one of his best and wealthiest customers who brought him a lot of business and changed cars every few years? Certainly not "no."

Dad got to see the entire USA with all expenses paid plus a salary greater than he made at work, simply for expressing sincere concern for a person's feelings on a road test. And this was during the Depression, when most people were out of work, much less traveling!

Dad was engaged to Mom at the time. After they married, Mrs. Spaulding always kept in touch. Thus, we enjoyed a special day each year for as long as she lived. Remember, a little empathy can go a long way.

Distractions——A Part Of Life

Take a few moments to reflect on how many times you have been involved with something important and had it all fall apart because of an interrupting distraction. If you cannot come up with several moments, my suggestion is to get some professional help. You must be out of touch with reality.

We have all heard of Murphy's Law. This obviously relates to things falling apart at the worst possible time. Not only do I know of Murphy's Law, it has happened so many times, it must be true!

You have to get somewhere fast and the car will not start. You have worked hard to cut down a tree and the chain breaks on the saw at a critical point. You have called an important client on your cell phone multiple times, and when you finally get through, you enter a "dead zone." If you were to keep it up, you could have one heck of a pity party. Call in a group of friends with this as your evening entertainment, and have a side ache from laughter before the beer and chips are gone!

When your career involves selling, it is a foregone conclusion that it will also include multiple appointments.

In no way possible can a salesperson be on his game 100 percent of the time. Most of the time, the good days will outweigh the bad. I would like to read about the salesperson who never faced distractions or had one put them off their game. Only read about them, because a meeting would be a waste of valuable time.

Again, I cannot recall the specific year; however, it is not important to this true story.

I had attained my final position and title of vice president, sales and marketing, as well as a member of the board. Along with this position came the responsibility of overseeing several key accounts of the business. Tuscan Dairy of Union, New Jersey was one of these accounts. Tuscan supplied us with a few specialty products we needed for distribution. In turn, we supplied them with some bulk cottage cheese. This "you scratch my back and I will scratch yours" approach to business is quite common in the dairy industry.

I had a scheduled appointment with their buyer late one morning to review sales on both sides of the operations as well as explore an opportunity for increased business. Tuscan was about 325 miles from our plant. I have always been a solid believer in the value of visiting other people's turf to see what they are doing better than we, as well as visiting future potential customers. Tuscan was a five-hour drive. After the appointment, I would visit several supermarkets on the way home, looking for new ideas. At the time, I was single. Spending a long day on the road and getting home in the middle of the night was not an issue at all.

Being a country boy and not accustomed to life in the big city, I planned my drive time a little too tight! On the Garden State Freeway, I calculated arrival with ten minutes to spare.

You could see the plant from the Garden State Union exit. I saw it, paid my toll, and breathed a sigh of relief. I got off at Vauxhall Road, turned right, and expected to arrive at the plant in one minute. Wrong! Next thing I knew, I was in the middle of a housing development. Starting to panic, I noticed a lady walking on the sidewalk clothed in a very stylish trench coat. I pulled up beside her, lowered the window, and asked, "Excuse me—can you give me directions to Tuscan?" I know now why men do not (or should not) stop to ask directions. She put her head through the window, saw I was neatly dressed, and said, "Tuscan! I ain't never heard of a Tuscan!" She stepped back from the window, pulled open her trench coat, and was as naked as the day she was born! She said, "I can't help you with Tuscan, but what else can I do for you?"

Well, up went the window, and off went I to find the place on my own. I found it with about two minutes to spare. Kind of stressed out, I made the meeting just in time. Do you think for one minute that I could fully concentrate on my presentation? Whenever there was a moment of silence, all I could picture was this attractive naked woman with her trench coat pulled open! I think (hope) the buyer thought my lack of focus was due to the lengthy drive from Maine and my fatigue from five hours on the road.

I did not accomplish a heck of a lot that day. The drive home was filled with fantasy and not related to business one iota!

Closing And Sound Business

No matter what the circumstance, the time will come when you should close the deal or give it your best shot. There is not a foolproof formula for this part of any presentation. It centers on timing and should occur as soon as you know the full interest of the prospect is in your hands. You can sense that they want to be part of the action. Do not ramble on; just bring it to a close, attain the proper signature, and graciously get out. Hanging around too long could easily result in the deal falling apart. Once the fuse is lit on a firecracker, it is no time to listen to the instructor explain how the noise could startle an innocent bystander. Toss the thing and run!

I recall the time years ago, when I finally closed the deal on an account I had worked on for more than a year. The buyer simply stated, "You have worked me over long enough. I am going to give you a shot. How soon can you start?"

On the way back to the dairy to process the paperwork, I was as excited as I can recall being in a long time. When I was walking the hall toward my office, I noticed the door of our chief financial officer, Don Brydon, was open. Unable to contain myself, I stepped into his office with a Cheshire cat grin and proceeded to tell him the story. Don listened to every word with the patience of a saint. When the story was complete, he simply looked at me and stated, "Dick, I am very happy for you; however, remember that from where I sit, the sale—no matter how large—is no good at all until the check clears and continues to clear the bank." This man was no fun at all!

In almost any business, there will be stories of "one-upmanship." Collections are not the average salesperson's strong point. Collection managers live on a breakfast diet of battery acid and nails. For lunch, they dine on legal soul food while in court, and for evening dessert, they chew on the ass of salesmen.

The following tough collection story again involves second-generation owner of Oakhurst, Don Bennett. Only an owner would probably go this far.

We had a summer camp account owner who managed to avoid payment for the majority of the season, with a list of all kinds of excuses. He had the money but did not want to part with it in any way. One day, Don, as owner of the dairy, drove his Cadillac to the camp unannounced to confront the camp owner with the bill. He met privately with him, and after much discussion, the camp owner reached for his checkbook. This figure is not correct, but I will say the bill was for $855.47. The camp owner handed Don a check for $855, stood up, and asked him to leave. Don looked at the check and said, "It is short by forty-seven cents." The camp owner went into a little tirade. Don simply sat down and waited. He informed the camp owner that he could easily rip up the check, call his attorney, and see him in court. The prestige and poor publicity for the camp owner would not be good for his business. He came up with the forty-seven cents and Don left. Like they sometimes say, "It is not the school that is bad, but the principle of the thing."

Closing a sale is fun; however, make sure all parties involved understand the payment arrangement.

Importance Of Prompt Follow-Up

There are so many times when good intentions are just not good enough. How often in personal and professional life have you told a person you would get back to them, but for whatever excuse failed to do so? When given serious thought, you will probably realize it was way too often. You got busy or distracted and quite honestly forgot your promise. Let me tell you up front that a salesperson making this mistake is probably doomed to disappointment. Being a good listener will help you jump many hurdles. Often a prospect is on the fence. They like what you say but are reluctant to make a decision. They may have sound reasoning for being on the fence. Most likely, there are other firms offering the same service. They also want this business. On top of that, you may be the least-known player in the field. A small slip-up on your part could prove costly.

The following true story is a classic example of prompt follow-up and how it landed a large account.

It is quite common in the dairy business for larger firms to bottle for others. A dairy may find itself in a position where the cost of production is too great for a satisfactory return on sales. It can remain in a profitable business and maintain its product identity, simply by having another firm private label for it. They in turn continue supplying other distributors, who broaden their market share. This works well for a distributor, as long as all remains well with the parent company.

We were supplying a few products to a moderately sized dairy out of state. This dairy also happened to have a very high-volume distributor. For reasons not important to this example, the dairy rapidly found itself in a position where continued production at their plant was no longer an option. Overnight, this put his large distributor in a bind to rapidly find a replacement supply of product.

Again, this was no small distributor. He was well known to several very large firms, who would grab his business in a heartbeat. Out of courtesy to Oakhurst, he called me to state his position and the fact that he was going to make a new supplier decision very shortly. The only reason we were called is because he happened to sell a few of the products we supplied and thought we should know it would probably go away.

Mike Crimmins is the owner of this distributorship. He is a hands-on owner who also runs a route of his own. He goes to work by 5 AM six days per week and is rarely finished and on his way home before nightfall.

I asked Mike if he would meet with me at a restaurant in Portsmouth, New Hampshire after work that evening to at least hear my pitch regarding Oakhurst. He said fine, but it would be a short meeting, because he had to get home for a little sleep before getting up at 4 AM and going off to work again.

When we met, I sensed he had already pretty much made up his mind regarding a new supplier. He was such an important distributor that the owner of a very large and well-established dairy in New England had been personally calling him to work out details and solidify his business.

However, I also sensed he was impressed that I had taken the time after a day's work to drive to New Hampshire to meet him. We were getting along fine. When he asked me some specific details regarding a couple products we manufactured, I had to honestly tell him I only knew the generalities and would have to get back to him. He basically said, "Thanks. Give me a call when you can."

I left the meeting with him around 9:00 PM. I drove the hour back to our plant in Portland, Maine, found answers to the specific issues he questioned, obtained samples of the products, and went home. At 2:00 AM, I got out of bed and drove to his facility location at the New Hampshire-Massachusetts border. I was waiting when he showed up for work, complete with all the answers to his questions as well as samples. Needless to say, Mike was impressed. I assured him I would be his personal contact and could meet whatever criteria were required for the transition. I do not think he had ever met a company executive who took this much personal interest.

We obtained the business. Why? Immediate follow-up on issues that may have been perceived as small. To this day, I feel that if the owner of the competitive large dairy had taken the time to visit Mike and not just call him, we would not have been successful.

Treat Customers Like Gold

At the outset, I focused on the fact that each individual is unique. We harbor feelings and react to circumstances in an individual manner. At any given time, I have no idea what you may be personally thinking, any more than you may know my thoughts.

As Americans, it is awesome that we can argue, debate, and poke fun at national (or any) leaders, knowing it is within our rights to do so. It is also awesome in troubled times how we put feelings aside, join together, and unite as the most unified and generous people on the planet. When we step into a voting booth, we vote however we feel. You might have voted one way, yet state another! Tom Zucal, a friend of mine from New Jersey, has often stated, "I hand wrote a vote for Abraham Lincoln, because a dead guy is better than anything running now!"

When it comes to customers, I take serious issue when all I hear is what a jerk they are. I constantly reminded employees that without those "jerks," they would not have a paycheck. If you were stupid enough to sign them up as a customer, then be smart enough to realize that the problem is yours. Spend the same amount of time trying to win over the jerk as you do complaining and you just might find another increase in profitability with somebody you already serve!

I know and accept the fact that remaining profitable in business often requires changing service or even dropping some customers. Like it or not, time is money. One should not overspend to maintain a situation that is costly. That is, unless your whole focus in life is the maintenance of a boat! Then you have (as the expression goes) "a hole in the water that sucks up cash." And you keep it. Dumb American!

One of the most gut-wrenching times I can recall occurred in the 1970s, when the company realized it could no longer remain in the home delivery business. For decades, home delivery of dairy products was as natural as apple pie. The milkman was such an icon, he (or she) was considered a part of the customer's family. It was common for a customer to leave a house key for the milkman to "keep an eye on the place" while the family was on vacation.

As the economy began to shift, the number of stay-at-home moms decreased rapidly. They found jobs to help support the rising costs of raising a family. It was very easy to stop at the store on the way home. The benefit of home delivery went away for many. Also, when faced with a detailed milk bill each week, products were cut to keep the costs down. It became increasingly difficult to gain new customers, as well as to sell extras to the ones who remained. It is quite easy to loudly complain at the "horrible" total of a supermarket checkout bill. We all do it. When the dairy portion is hidden in the total, it does not appear to be the shock of a separate bill. We were working harder for a lot less return. A truck could leave more volume at one large supermarket or convenience store than a home-delivery salesperson could sell in a day.

Before it was over, we ceased delivery to 15,000 to 20,000 customers. It was not done overnight. We sent flyers to all customers, with coupons for free product that could legally be obtained at their favorite supermarket or convenience store. The home-delivery salespersons made personal visits as much as possible to explain what was going to occur and why. We absorbed as many jobs as possible in the plant and new wholesale routes. We worked hard in the community to find work for several employees.

In the end, we managed to maintain the trust and confidence of our customers, and they continued supporting us by purchasing our products at the store. It was a very difficult but necessary period in the history of the company. Only by reaching out on a personal basis to let our customers know how much they meant were we able to accomplish the goal with positive results.

In this modern age of computerization, all businesspeople have been forced to adapt to their importance. This is change at its best. I can only wonder what the future of business communication will be in 100 years. No matter what occurs, the wise and astute leader will learn how to use this knowledge to reflect personal involvement.

There is an expression that a good deed will be only passed on to three people, while a poor deed will be passed on to ten. As a leader, always remember that the small player may one day become a large one. If you treated the small with respect, it could pay large future dividends. Conversely, if you become slack with the large, you may well end up on the outside looking in.

I recall late one afternoon my phone rang with an extremely small customer who ran a restaurant on the other end. His business was thirty miles from the plant. Our route salesman just plain skipped his delivery that day because the order was so small. He decided not to waste his time with such nonsense.

The customer simply told me that we had put him in a bind, and he was now going to have to send an employee to a distant market to purchase milk needed later that evening. He said something like, "Thanks for misleading the public with all your claims of goodness." He hung up.

Our routes were in. People had gone home. I was just working late on a contract. After the call, I could not concentrate on anything. I called him back, stating that he would have his product in one hour, and not to send anyone to the store.

I called shipping, got the single case of milk, tossed it in a cooler in my car, and took off for his restaurant. When I got there, he was still upset. He asked who I was. I told him, "Vice president of a company that owes you a personal apology." I gave him the product at no charge, went into his dining room, and ordered an expensive entrée, and insisted paying full price. When I left, he thanked me. Obviously, the route salesman and I came to a mutual understanding the next day.

Treat customers like gold. Without them, all you have is a plan and a dream.

Determination

An old 1986 edition of *Webster's Dictionary* describes determination as follows: "the act or process of determining fixed purpose: resolution: adherence to a definite line of action."

The last statement, "adherence to a definite line of action," is most important. Every person will display degrees of determination throughout his or her life; however, a salesperson lacking this characteristic is bound for failure.

We bump into people every day who are determined to make an ass of themselves. We bump into people every day who are determined to win. We bump into people every day who are determined to make a statement, either good or bad. We can bump into people who are able to accomplish all three in the same day. In this story, I was such a person!

Fishing is an adventure revered by most Americans. It is a way of life for many. For most, it is assigned the prestigious title of recreation therapy. It is an American rite of passage. To many it is a more popular avocation than baseball, football, and perhaps to one or two off-the-wall types, even sex.

For nearly fifteen years of my adult single life, I was fortunate enough to live six months per year on my boat located at Brewer's South Freeport Marine. Brewer's is located at the shore of the Harraseeket River, a part of Casco Bay, and only a couple miles from the world-famous L.L. Bean sporting goods parent store.

It is nearly impossible to live on a boat on the ocean and not be involved with fishing. I was certainly involved, yet quickly developed the reputation as one of the worst enthusiasts to ever wet a line. If fishing were to be my source of income, I would have starved long ago. The state would not have had a problem, as I would have been too weak and undernourished to collect a welfare check. I had all the gear and advice. Fish just would not cooperate!

Each summer featured the annual striped bass and bluefish tournament. It was a two-day event with wonderful prizes. Serious fishermen take to the ocean, determined to win a significant prize in at least one of several categories. One summer weekend during the 1990s, I decided it was time for me to demonstrate how it was done.

It was going to be my personal getaway weekend. Nothing but me, my boat, and the thrill of two days on the ocean with "man against the elements." In preparation, I even think I re-read Hemingway's *The Old Man and the Sea*.

The home base for the tournament was beside the Kennebec River in Bath, Maine. Bath is famous for its rich history of shipbuilding, and is the home of Bath Ironworks. This firm is the state's largest employer and a prime builder of destroyers for the U.S. Navy.

Early on, I registered and established my game plan. The strategy was to leave Brewer's at daylight and fish all day, ending at Boothbay Harbor for an overnight. The next morning, I would leave Boothbay Harbor and fish most of the day and end my fishing at the weigh-in station at Bath. I would turn in my trophy catch, collect my prize money, and cruise the twenty-five miles back to Brewer's with bragging rights and a trophy to prove same! This is a serious weekend. I estimated the cost of fuel for the boat, plus overnight slip fee in Boothbay, two days of food, entrance fee, and fishing supplies to be in excess of $400 ... plus alcohol!

I already owned tons of fishing gear; however, for something as special as this, I drove the two miles from the boat to L.L. Bean's store in Freeport and looked up a fishing clerk for some advice. The man was wonderful, and very good for L.L. Bean, as he convinced me I should purchase a lure almost guaranteed to catch bluefish. That was okay, but the lure cost ten dollars! In the 1990s, ten bucks was a lot of money for one lure. I bought it.

As planned, early Saturday morning, I loosed my lines from the dock, and *Dad's Pad* (name of my boat) and I were off on an adventure. Just outside the river, I set two lines and trolled nearly seven miles to Mackerel Cove on Bailey Island for a quick coffee and muffin breakfast break. No luck, but the coffee and muffin were delicious.

From there, I set the lines again and trolled all the way to the mouth of the Kennebec River. From Bailey Island, it was a distance of about ten miles. Still no luck; however, I did not mind, as the weather was perfect for offshore cruising: bright sunshine, light winds, with mild ocean swells.

At the mouth of the Kennebec, I stopped at Fort Popham to walk around and stretch my legs. Then I was off again, fishing the Kennebec to Bath. Still no luck! At Bath, I stopped for lunch before heading to Boothbay Harbor. The boat trip from Bath to Boothbay via the Sasanoa River is one of the most beautiful cruises on the coast of Maine. In certain sections, the river is quite narrow. The current can be severe during flood tide. No matter; I love this passage. It passes through a wildlife sanctuary, crosses Hockomock Bay, enters Knubble Bay, proceeds through Goose Rock Passage, and ends at the Sheepscot River. You then cross the Sheepscot River and proceed to Boothbay Harbor via the Southport Swing Bridge. From Bath, it is another ten-mile trip to Boothbay Harbor and the end of day one. I had not a single bite for the whole day!

I docked *Dad's Pad* at Boothbay Harbor Marina and spent the evening pigging out on junk food, gin and tonic, and a few local brews. Still not discouraged, I staggered back to the boat for a decent night's sleep and great hopes for the morrow!

Early Sunday morning, it was the same drill: coffee and muffin at a local restaurant, and then back to sea. For day two, I decided to reverse my course and proceed up the Sasanoa to Bath and fish until weigh-in time.

I had two lines out and fishing upstream through a fast-flowing current at Goose Rock Passage and Knubble Bay. The current was running strongly, and I had to stay in a tight channel around some marker buoys.

At the worst possible time, behind me I heard the rapid "zing" of one fishing line spinning wildly off the spool. Most fishermen, when they hear this sound, just about come unglued and nearly wet their pants. I was more focused on keeping the boat in the channel. I knew that the zinging line was the pole with my ten-dollar L.L. Bean lure. Quickly, I shifted the engine to neutral and looked behind me, expecting to see the line and fish jumping wildly off the stern. I knew I would have to rapidly tighten the drag to prevent the line from running to the end and breaking off the spool.

The problem was this: The line was not in the water off the stern of the boat. The line was thirty feet in the air and spinning out rapidly with a huge seagull at the end. I set the drag a little stronger on the reel, grabbed my second pole, and started to reel it in before it got tangled in the prop. The boat was rapidly moving in the current toward certain danger beyond a channel marker.

Putting the engine back in gear, I was able to maneuver the boat with the current until it reached calmer waters in Goose Rock Passage. Now I was able to put the engine in neutral again and concentrate on reeling in the second line before dealing with the seagull. The seagull was now forty feet in the air and flapping wildly!

The basic rules of this situation dictate that I cut the line and let nature deal with the seagull and its dilemma. Rules be darned! That seagull had my ten-dollar L.L. Bean lure in its mouth and there was no way I would let that go. So with boatloads of people watching, and cameras clicking, and other fishermen popping open a beer to witness the event, I began the long process of reeling in a big seagull fifty yards behind me and forty feet in the air. I am sure you have all witnessed fishermen on yachts, sitting in a big chair and reeling in a huge tuna. They extend the pole straight out in front of them, slowly pull it up over their head, and then rapidly reel in the line while letting the pole go back to the extended position. Thus, the fish gets closer to the boat. It is eventually tired out and then hooked with a gaff and brought on board. I had no large seat, but was doing the same with the seagull. The dumb bird had no intention of coming aboard without a fight.

The seagull was both tough and strong. I worked it for about fifteen minutes before it came close to the boat, wings flapping like mad, and screeching with an awful AAWK-AAWK sound.

Another dilemma! How am I going to land this thing without getting myself all beat up and perhaps even hooked with my own L.L. Bean ten-dollar lure? Time to think it over. I did not want to kill the bird, for a lot of reasons. Number one, it was illegal. Number two, I am such a softy when it comes to injured animals, I once rescued an injured gull by the highway and drove it all the way to the Animal Refuge League for help. It had a broken wing. The staff regarded me as some kind of fool and promptly put the gull in a vacuum chamber and ended it all.

With one hand holding the pole with the seagull near the tip going wild, I reached for my trusty hammer used for bonking bluefish I might catch, and proceeded to reach out and give the seagull a little "tunk" on the head. Bluefish have very sharp teeth and a reputation for being ferocious when caught. Placing your hand near the mouth of one could easily cause the loss of fingers.

I managed to just daze the seagull. I grabbed it by the neck, put it on the floor, took my trusty pliers, and extracted my ten-dollar L.L. Bean lure.

People in other boats near me were still taking pictures, laughing, and drinking beer. I splashed water onto the seagull's head, and after a while, it began to wake up and shake its head from side to side. When I felt it was somewhat roused, I tossed it over the stern and back into the sea. The last I saw of the bird, it was dunking its head in and out of the water like bobbing for apples.

I had spent more than four hundred dollars, and only had the landing of a seagull for all my efforts. Trust me; I was very tempted to take the gull in a sack to the weigh-in. If I had, I surely would have been arrested and faced a huge fine. If the tournament had a class for "flying fish," I would have entered it in the category for widest wingspan!

What did I prove by all of this? (1) Determination to save my ten-dollar L.L. Bean lure at any cost. (2) Determination to win no matter what. (3) Proof that I could make an ass of myself in the process. If given the opportunity, would I do it all over again? YES—YES—YES.

Leave With A Positive Thought

When you walk away from a sales presentation, it may have resulted in a win-lose-draw. In my mind, it is also very important that you leave the meeting with a memorable positive thought. Why? It may be the only real thing that the prospect remembers. Never forget that you are not the only person bidding for their attention and time. He or she probably has scheduled meetings all day long. Several may be with people offering the same type of service you do.

I am not talking about trivial comments such as "I hope we can do business soon," or "You are in charge of a magnificent firm and it would be an honor for us to partner with you." These types of closing remarks are a dime a dozen and leave no more impression than the boring store clerk whose only comment is "How are you today?" You say "fine," no matter how you feel. Not me. I make some comment like "Glad to be looking at the ground from the top!" I would like to say, "You look quite pale. Do you think you will live through the remainder of your shift?"

My entire career was devoted to "the dairy business." As already discussed, during that tenure I was able to witness an industry grow, consolidate, and change with amazing speed. The only real problem is that it continues to remain quite flat regarding per-capita consumption. If it had not been for the introduction of flavored milks, attractive packaging, and increased shelf life, milk sales nationwide would be quite dismal. It is "nature's most perfect food." It should be an important part of nutritional intake for as long as we live. Why does the demand for milk rapidly decrease when one reaches teenage years and adulthood?

There have been millions in research devoted to this very question. It ends up with novel marketing approaches such as the "milk mustache" program and others to convince us we never outgrow our need for milk. These are excellent programs, and they do have a limited and positive impact on sales. Great! However, sales remain flat with the general population.

I am a solid believer in the "KISS" principle, which simply means "keep it simple, stupid." I have a very simple theory that if correct will make a fortune for the first company to solve the problem. Why do people stop drinking significant amounts of milk? Very simply, as "dumb Americans," we only like our milk when it is very *cold*.

When we were very young, Mom and Dad could force it on us, no matter what. All one needs to do today is visit school lunchrooms and determine the age when kids start drinking very little or none of their milk. They stick with the chocolate longest of all because the flavor helps overcome the objection. The amount of milk wasted daily in lunchrooms is appalling! By the time it is ready to drink, it is too warm! A person will drink a whole glass of water before a whole carton of milk. Why? Warm water is not objectionable any more than lukewarm soda or "bug juice."

I am an adult who consumes more milk than the average person my age; however, I dislike warm milk and often toss it before finishing when driving in the car trying to enjoy a sandwich and beverage. Warm or cool coffee or soda will get consumed no matter what!

My challenge to not only the firm from which I retired but also the whole industry is to solve this problem. Then you have something to market with a story all your own!

I am from the state of Maine, where there is more water than one can imagine; and thinking one day bottled water would become the best-selling liquid in the nation was well beyond any consideration of common sense I could fathom. Today, bottled water sales are number one! Price is not the issue! Frequently, I watch people pay $1.49 for a small container.

Water is the highest base ingredient of milk and it has so much more nutritional value!

Do not just think about it. Make it happen!

On page one, I stated that we are all salesmen, as well as being unique individuals with thoughts special only to us.

If you were to gain nothing more from my personal sales motivation technique stories than to stimulate a self-examination of your personal goals, then I have succeeded.

I have shared a small fraction of my life story. Now think about yours and make it become whatever you desire! In the race of life, there are no losers, just lost opportunities.